Tips to Improve Your Retirement Experience

By Ray Matlock Smythe

Preface

The purpose of this book is to give potential retirees and folks already retired some new ideas, plans, and perspectives on how to have a fun, marvelous, and rewarding retirement. I have included my ideas along with some guest writers to give their words of wisdom. I also included some fascinating quotes about retirement. This book does not have economic advice as that can come from a financial planner. I am hoping the ideas in my book will help you to have a more serene, relaxed, and fulfilling retirement. Have a great read!

Dedication

I am dedicating this book to the following people because I am impressed and inspired by the way they are living their retirement years:

Sharon Hagedorn

Ron Hagedorn

Ruth Gregg

Doug Halm

Bill McClintock

Ron Krueger

Susan Krueger

Ron Meier

Davis Moriuchi

Judy Moriuchi

Monte Johnston

Elaine Johnston

Acknowledgements

Special thanks to Steve Oliver for all of his wise advice in the publishing and writing of this book. His editing skills were excellent and his encouragement was very much appreciated.

Thank you also to Brian Bachant (The Desert Print Shop, Cathedral City, CA) for working with me on this third book. I am grateful for his kindness and generous help. He made the cover and produced the book.

Walk, Walk, Walk

Walking is the absolute best thing you can do every day. Study after study says that walking each day for thirty minutes helps your heart, your lungs, your bones, and your attitude. You feel better both mentally and physically. Keeping motivated to walk is the problem. So the best solution for motivation is to walk with a friend or a group of friends.

We have a walking group in our neighborhood. It has been around for fifteen years. Our group is called the WAGS (Walking And Gossiping Society). We walk two miles each day. We even have tee shirts that have a logo on them and we wear them on Mondays. Every other year, we order new shirts with different colors. It is fun to have the shirts. After our two mile walk, we go back to the same house for coffee. We all bring coffee and creamers so the host house does not have to spend a fortune on coffee.

Some days at coffee we have serious talks about politics and health. Having said that, most days we are simply silly and joking around. It is a wonderful way to start the day. Many members say it is the best part of their day. It is the combination of exercise and a sense of belonging that keeps the walking group going. The camaraderie of the group is wonderful.

So start a walking program for yourself, your family, or your friends when you retire. It will not only keep you healthy, but it will keep you socially active.

Back to College

It is fun to go back to school. The Osher Lifelong Learning Institute is a program for adults age 50 and above. It offers university level classes with a huge range of subjects. Presently, there are 118 institutes at universities in 50 states. There are no tests and no homework assignments. Classes are presented simply for the joy of learning. It doesn't get any better than this program.

Would you like to learn conversational Spanish? How about hearing about near-death experiences? What about studying the history of the troubled Middle East? Visualize seeing classic masterpieces during an art appreciation class. The list of subjects and classes are truly endless.

Most doctors agree that keeping the mind active as we age is one of the most important ways to prevent dementia and Alzheimer's disease. The mind needs to be stimulated on a variety of subjects. It keeps people living in the present. The Osher Institute is a nonprofit program that keeps folks enthusiastic about learning new things.

Now your city or town may not have an Osher Program. If not, sign up for classes at your local senior center or community college. There are many classes for seniors these days. You will not only learn new information, but you will meet people. I can't begin to tell you what a difference going back to school has made in my life. I love it! That is why I am telling you now. Go back to school as it is both educational and entertaining .

Learn to Play a Musical Instrument

Everyone loves some kind of music. Most people reading this book probably like either classical, popular, country, or rock and roll. It really doesn't matter what you like, but how about learning something new? How about learning how to play that instrument you always wanted to learn, but never had the time?

My friend, Johanne Verville learned to play the ukulele at the age of 68. She had always wanted to learn to play this and she finally took it up. Now she goes to the beach each weekend. She plays the ukulele with about 150 other players on Friday nights at the local ocean pier. She says it is awesome to hear this huge group of people all playing the same instrument at once. Johanne is now teaching her nephew and niece how to play.

Do you want to learn to play a musical instrument? Perhaps it is the saxophone with its jazzy tones or maybe the violin with its strings echoing classical pieces of music. The piano is always a favorite as well. It doesn't matter. Go for it now.

Johanne said it best, " If I can learn to play the ukulele at the age of 68, anyone can. " So start practicing and who knows, you may even join a band or an orchestra.

Move To A New Place

I spent my first 50 years living in rainy, cloudy, and cool Portland, Oregon. It was beautiful when the sun came out, but there were over two hundred plus days of clouds. So when I retired, I decided to move to a sunny climate. I moved to Palm Springs, California.

Leaving Portland meant abandoning life-long friends, family members, and co-workers. It was tough, but guess what? Now all of those people come down here to the desert to visit me each year. I never had visitors in Portland, but the folks from Portland never stop coming down to relax in the sunny desert now.

I need to give you a cautionary note as this point. Do your research ahead of time. The worst thing you could do is move to a new location and then find out it is not right for your health or lifestyle. I had vacationed many years in Palm Springs and even had a condo here. So I knew the culture, the climate, and the people ahead of time. It was a great fit for me.

So visit your new city or state many times before you take the leap of leaving your home city. Many people choose to live in two places during retirement. They live in one home for the winter months and another home for the hot months. This is a fun way to live, but one has to have the money to afford it. However, as we all age, sometimes going back and forth between two places becomes too tiresome. Just the same, moving to a new place after you retire is so much fun. Your new home offers you new adventures, people, and experiences. I have never regretted my move to the desert. If you choose to move, I hope you have the same positive experience that I have had.

Go Out to Dinner

When I was working, I never had much energy or time to eat out. I would come home exhausted. All I wanted was to have some peace and quiet. I should state that I was a middle and high school history teacher. I loved my job, but being around teenagers all day was draining. So we usually ate at home and went to bed early.

Now that we are retired, we are free as a bird to stay up as late as we want or to retire as early as we desire. I like to eat early and now we go out many nights during the week. We try a variety of different restaurants. So a new Indian place opened and we tried their spicy curry dishes. A new bistro opened with half prices during happy hour for sliders and drinks. We like the place and have gone back often. Our favorite Thai food eatery moved to a new location. We like the place and visit it often.

The point is that we try a variety of places. Plus, we watch for the coupons and happy hour prices. Some places have prefix dinners for less than $20.00 so we patronize those restaurants.

Eating out has another huge advantage. It gives you an opportunity to socialize with other folks. Most of the time, we call up another couple and meet them at a particular place. By meeting your friends at restaurants, you stay connected and in the loop of what is going on in your community. It is always easier to meet people for breakfast, lunch, or dinner rather than have them over to your home. So let someone else do the cooking and go out today for a meal.

Naps

When you worked, you never had the time or opportunity for a nap. However, one of the great joys of retirement is being able to take a nap every afternoon. Many retirees have sleep problems. Doctors say we don't get enough sleep. I have a nurse friend who says that sleep is the best healer. So naps are a good thing.

I try and take a nap every day right after lunch. When your stomach is full, it helps you to fall asleep. Some people take a thirty minute nap and others take over an hour. Most doctors think the shorter naps are better, but I think you should listen to your own body. We are not all the same so nap according to how you feel.

I do suggest that when you wake up, you sit by the side of your bed for a minute before getting up. It just helps you to get your balance a bit more. If you have a dog or a cat, they will get into the habit of napping with you. My dog actually jumps onto the bed ahead of me signaling that is time for our nap!

Television

I don't watch a lot of the new television shows. Yes, there are some terrific shows and a mini - series like Downton Abby is a must to enjoy. I like to watch old television shows. One of my favorites is Perry Mason. So I have recorded all of those shows. Many times a week, I turn on a Perry Mason and enjoy it thoroughly. I never get tired of them and now I can stay up as late as I want to watch them and not worry about going to work the next morning.

So you can do the same. Start recording the shows you always enjoyed and begin watching them. Of course, you probably already are recording current shows and watching them at your leisure.

I don't watch television in my bedroom. I know many folks have sets in their bedrooms, but for me personally it works better to watch television in a den or living room. Also, if I have a television on in my bedroom it distracts me from getting good sleep.

Now that you are retired, watch those programs you always enjoyed. You have lots of time now to enjoy them.

Crossword Puzzles

Enjoy doing your favorite newspaper crosswords. I have several friends who just love doing their crosswords. As a matter of fact, their mornings start out by walking two miles and then returning home to start their crossword puzzles. One of them had been an NBC executive and had never had time to do them while he was working. Now, he just loves sipping his coffee and working on one each morning.

Another popular retirement activity related to crosswords are the Sudoku puzzles in the paper. I know that many folks enjoy these as well. Whether it is the daily newspaper crossword or the Sudoku puzzle, it is not only fun, but an excellent activity to stimulate your brain.

Massage

Do you know anyone who doesn't have aches and pains in their retirement years? Well, it is that time of life where our bodies take longer to heal and don't move as fast. One of the best treatments you can give yourself is a full body massage.

Massage has been around for hundreds of years. It helps wring out all of those sore muscles and ligaments. It not only feels good, but it is healthy for your body to release all of those toxins in your system. Your health is number one during these retirement years and massage will help keep you healthy.

It is important to find the right massage therapist. Some therapists apply too much pressure or others not enough. Personally, I like a therapist with whom I can connect intellectually with as well. My massage therapist is named Steve. He uses a strong amount of pressure and I like that as I have very sore muscles from sitting at a desk and computer all day. He is also quite the conversationalist. I like to talk during my massage and so does he. However, many folks want total quiet. So you will have to decide what works best for you and give that feedback to your therapist.

Jim Rohn wrote, " Take care of your body. It's the only place you have to live." Regular massages will keep your body free of toxins, help relieve pain, and make you feel refreshed. So put massages on the top of your list as an activity during your retirement years.

USO

Most large cities have a USO next to their airports. This organization is really wonderful for all of our young soldiers. If you are looking for a rewarding volunteer activity, this is it.

My friend Ron has volunteered for the local chapter here in Palm Springs. This USO is very active with soldiers going to and from the base at Twenty Nine Palms which is northeast of Palm Springs. They sponsor barbeques and picnics for the soldiers, prepare sandwiches, and supply cold soft drinks. They give them a place to sleep and toiletries as well.

Sometimes the soldiers just need someone to listen to them or give them some advice. Many of these soldiers are just young kids that are nineteen or twenty years old. They miss their families and need an older adult to guide them with some wise words or comforting thoughts. So if you are a veteran you would be a good candidate for helping at the USO. If you are not a veteran, you are still very welcome to volunteer. They need anyone who feels compassion for the men and women that keep our country free.

Home Organization

Retirement is best when you are organized. This means getting your bedroom, office, kitchen, and living room cleaned up and rid of clutter.

Our bedroom closets are full of clothes we will never wear again. We are not working nine to five and don't need those fancy clothes any longer. So go through your closets and drawers. Get rid of old clothes that no longer fit or are not in style. Purge your bedroom of everything you don't need.

Living here in the hot desert, I threw out two thirds of my long sleeved shirts and long pants. I basically only wear shorts and short sleeved shirts. It freed up my closet for storage.

If you have a home office, I am sure that keeping it clean and organized is an on-going project. My theory is that the office is fine until the mail comes each day. Then you begin to open your mail and slowly things morph into paper chaos no matter how hard you try to prevent it.

I recently read an article that said you should clean out and organize everything at the same time. It suggested that you start with something like books. If you haven't read them in a year, you probably never will, so give them away. Only keep books that you have read and that brought you joy. Take this advice for everything in your house that is causing clutter and mess. If it makes you feel good and brings you joy, keep it. If not, give it away or throw it away.

Letter Writing

I believe that living with an attitude of gratitude is the key to happiness. A rewarding activity to do regularly is write letters of gratitude to family and friends. Take the time to write your best friend, co-worker, neighbor, or family member telling them why you love them or find them so special. These are the types of letters that people keep for a lifetime. I have had many students and friends write me such letters and it was an absolute high. You feel so validated when someone writes you an unsolicited note.

When you were working, you didn't have the time or energy, but now you do. The letter will make you feel good, but it will be thrilling for your special person to receive it. I remember getting an awesome letter from my father when I was in my forties. He told me how proud he was of me and that he loved me. I still have the letter in my desk. So if you are a parent, you may want to write to your adult daughter or son and tell them how you feel about them.

I have even written letters to my doctors, dentists, teachers, car mechanics, and my hair cutter. It not only makes them feel good, but I feel great letting them know they are talented and special. Try it and you will get the same result.

Change Careers

Now that you are retired, you can pursue that other career you put on hold or try something you have always wanted to do. Basically, you re-invent yourself.

I have had several friends who held positions as important administrators in large companies who came down here to the desert and became receptionists or store clerks. They just wanted something fairly simple to do that didn't require them to take work home.

I have had many other friends who decided to work part - time during their retirement years. They found jobs as real estate agents, handy men, landscapers, or many other careers. I even worked part time as a teacher when I retired. I taught a couple of classes in the mornings and then had my afternoons free.

This book is about retirement, but some folks like to be partially retired. Again, you must do what is most comfortable for you. Some folks ask why you are still working , but as my friend Johanne says, "Why not, if you enjoy it? "

So if you want to change careers now is the time to do it. If you want to work part time in another career, now is the time to do it. If you want to investigate other options, now is the time to do it.

Paul Coelho stated, " One day you will wake up and there won't be any more time to do the things you've always wanted. Do it now." Please take his advice to heart.

Dogs

If you don't plan to travel a lot during your retirement years, get a dog. They are wonderful on every level. First, they bring love into any home. Two, they are healthy for you. Most people that have dogs are healthier than those who have none. Why? When you pet a dog or have a dog on your lap, your blood pressure goes down. Many dog owners walk their dogs every day so both you, the owner and your pooch get some exercise.

Police tell me that having a dog is an excellent deterrent for criminals wanting to burglarize your home. A barking dog is the last thing a robber wants to hear. Plus, if you have a hearing problem, your dog always lets you know when someone is at the front door.

Most of all, dogs bring you unconditional love. Where can you get that kind of love in today's society? Our retirement years are wonderful and fulfilling, but they can also be sprinkled with heavy doses of illness and sadness. A sudden death of a friend or family member is challenging to deal with anytime. Having a loyal dog companion helps to lessen the grieving process.

You are rich if you have a dog. Again, if you like to stay close to home, get a dog and enjoy many years of caring companionship.

Cats

I recommend having cats if you plan to do lots of traveling. Cats are much easier and more independent than dogs. They can stay alone for several days if you have a trusted person come to the house each day. This person can change the water and put out fresh food. The litter box can be cleaned and the cats are in good shape.

Cats seem to be able to withstand absences of humans easier than dogs. However, if you are going to be gone for a long time, I would recommend either a reputable house/cat sitter or have them boarded at a responsible pet boarding facility.

The bottom line for both cats and dogs is you need one that fits your lifestyle.

Read, Read, Read

My friends Judy and Davis read books like some people eat candy. They can't read enough and go through books as if there was no tomorrow. Most of us didn't have lots of time to read books when we were working. Now that we have extra time, we can read many books.

My problem is setting the time aside for reading. Many times I start thinking about " projects " I should be doing like cleaning the garage or taking old clothes to the local charity. It is a good idea to just set aside some time that works for you to simply read. I like to read in the afternoons or early evening. I don't watch a lot of television these days and it is quite relaxing to have a dog on my lap with a good book in my hands.

Besides being fun, reading keeps you informed about the world. It also helps as a conversation starter when you are at a party or having coffee with folks. People like to know what you are reading and like to share.

I started a Book Club when I moved here to the desert. We met once a month and it was fun to hear people's opinions about different books. The host of the month would provide drinks and appetizers. We would discuss the book and then vote on a new one for the following month. The meeting would last about an hour and a half. So that is an activity that some of your readers might start in your town or city. Again, this is something that keeps your mind active and alert.

Cruises

I believe cruising is the easiest way to travel these days. You get to the ship, unpack once, and you are home free. No hunting for a hotel, no worries about where to eat, and no wondering where to visit next. It is all taken care of for you and the itinerary is set ahead of time.

There are so many activities on all of the cruise ships these days. One has everything from BINGO games, weight training, to Alcoholics Anonymous Meetings. There are wonderful Las Vegas style shows at night and dancing to the wee hours of the morning.

Cruising isn't for everyone. Some people feel too confined being on a ship for a week or two or perhaps feel claustrophobic in the small cabins. However, I believe most people enjoy having their beds made up for them every night and all the extra's cruise lines do for their passengers these days.

I have been on many cruises through the years and I have to say the one that I enjoyed so many times was not in Europe or the Caribbean. It was the cruise to Alaska. The scenery is simply stunning. The snow - capped mountains, the wildlife, the small towns, and floating ice fields are spectacular. So I would definitely recommend cruising as an easy way to have a vacation.

Golf

My friend, Michael Pettit talked to me about golfing. He learned to play golf at the age of 55. One of the reasons he loves golf is for the exercise. Everything you read states that exercise of any kind is imperative for retirees to stay healthy. Michael says he sees people in their 90's out on the course. They are swinging their clubs to hit the ball, walking on the greens, and getting in and out of carts. They are not sitting in their living rooms watching television, but out on the golf course moving.

Golf is also excellent for the mind as you are always calculating strategies for how to best hit the ball. You try to decide which club will work best for the desired result. As a golfer, you try to judge distances for your shots. So the mind is constantly being used. This is most important to prevent diseases like dementia.

Most doctors believe that physical activity, socialization, and good nutrition are the components to keep seniors healthy and alive. Golf does all of the above.

Michael feels that the best thing golf does for him is give him a total distraction from everything in life. It clears his mind of daily living as you are only concentrating on one thing. You basically leave everything else behind for three hours.

Golf has been a real joy for Michael and millions of other folks in America. Now that you are retired, you have plenty of time to enjoy this wonderful game.

Being Invisible

My friend Elaine says she feels invisible now that she is retired. Her belief is that often you feel as if you are no longer valued as a contributing member of society. It is as if your opinion does not count any longer or you are considered an " old person " or a " geezer." This propels retired folks into a depression. Worse than the depression, it makes some retirees feel like they are " less than " a whole person.

Many retirees equated their worth and importance with their jobs. It didn't matter if you were a doctor, teacher, plumber, or a street sweeper as you had a position in society. You got paid for doing something. You could tell people what you did eight hours a day. When you quit that career, you no longer can tell people about your job.

Thus, it is imperative that all retirees have a plan for their retirement years. You must set goals for things or activities you want to accomplish. They can be simple things like walking for thirty minutes each day or grander plans like climbing Mt. Everest. The point is you need a plan and a set of goals. However, you would be more successful to write your goals out and post them where you can see them each day. Most successful people say that posting the goals and seeing them often aids them in meeting their goals.

So begin today to set some small and larger goals for your retirement years. It is no fun feeling invisible. When you have a map of where you want to go then you will no longer feel like you are adrift in society. Richard Halliburton (writer and adventurer) once said, " Live the wonderful life that is in you. Be afraid of nothing."

Eyes

Let's face it.....our eyes are not as good as they were when we were young. So it is important to have a good maintenance plan for our eyes. This means regular appointments to the eye doctor. It is a challenge to enjoy simple things like reading the paper, if your eyes are not working well. It is also dangerous as well. If you can't see to drive, don't drive. Have someone drive you to the eye doctor and find out what can be done to improve your eyesight.

I recently noticed that my right eye was not functioning correctly. As a matter of fact, I was having difficulty reading the big letters on the eye chart. Plus, driving at night was quite challenging. I made an appointment with my eye doctor. He discovered a cataract that was growing rapidly in my right eye. So we scheduled a surgery date and I had a new lens put in my eye. What a huge difference! It was like a small miracle. I could see better, colors were brighter, and everything was more defined. Cataract surgery is very common these days and one of the most successful surgeries around. So I highly recommend it when the time is right.

We often hear negative things about the aging process. However, eye surgery can reverse the aging process. People in their 70's and 80's can often see better after cataract surgery than their friends in their 40's and 50's. So be sure to keep on top of your vision as it is one thing about aging that can improve with proper care.

Booze

This is a difficult and challenging subject to discuss. As a baby boomer, I have partied as hard as the next person. However, when I was working, I limited my partying to the weekends as I had to work during the weekdays.

Retirement erases that barrier of abstinence during the week. Now you can drink every day and not have to worry about getting up and performing at work. Of course, that is a new problem. No responsibility for work, no responsibility for drinking whenever you want to now. It is easy to start the cocktail hour at four o'clock in the afternoon. You have some friends over and make some appetizers. Your party has started. The problem is that you get into the habit of drinking and then it becomes a lethal habit. You move the cocktail hour down to three o'clock or maybe begin at lunch. It suddenly goes from a habit to an addiction. One we all need to be aware of during retirement.

Maybe you can sustain your habit for several years, but eventually it will go sour. You start killing too many brain cells and you start having more senior moments. If you live in a 55+ community, many others will share this habit of drinking regularly and too much. Worse yet, if you are alone, you can develop the habit of drinking by yourself. Remember you are drinking poison as that is what gives you the high. It is also damaging your liver, kidneys, and other organs. I once asked my doctor about the benefits of red wine. He told me to drink a couple of glasses of grape juice to reap the same rewards. So my yellow caution light is to watch your drinking. It is easy to get carried away with Peggy Lee's old song, " Is That All There Is? " and break out the booze. Remember health is number one when we are getting older and drinking to excess will ruin your health.

Falls

I fell last Christmas day. I completely missed the cement front stair that goes up to the landing of my front door. The front door has black wrought iron security gates on it. I literally slammed my face full force into the rod iron gates, hitting my head and my right eye hard. I was a bloody mess, but escaped without any serious injuries. I was lucky.

I have had so many friends fall this past couple of years. They were all in their sixties, but simply did not see a curb or a stair. One friend really hurt his rotator cuff on his right shoulder. Another friend shattered her wrist causing her surgeon to put eleven screws in her hand. She is still recovering and will probably never achieve 100% of her former function.

The purpose of this page is to remind everyone our age that we can't afford a bad fall. No one needs a broken hip, leg, or arm during the retirement years. All of us must be conscious and present when we are going from one place to another. Never be afraid to ask for help on stairs.

It is imperative that we pay attention to our surroundings when we are walking. This means paying extra attention to ice, snow, and rain during the winter months. It also means holding on to railings when we are in buildings, going down stairways, or walking into restaurants. It also means hanging on to someone if our footing is a little off or we are not feeling 100%. It is also wise to assess your home for helpful aids like handrails in the shower or by the toilet.

Make it a yearly resolution to walk more carefully.

Living in the Moment

This is a very important topic. The purpose of this page is to live in the present moment. Some people simply say living in the now or in the present. Whatever you want to title it, live and stay in the moment. Others call it mindfulness or staying in the moment.

For example, let's say you are lunching with three good friends. You are all having a ball talking about your last get together or plans in the future. Suddenly you start thinking about a remark you made to your spouse yesterday. Did he/she take it the wrong way? Then you remember that in a week you are leaving on a Hawaiian vacation. You haven't packed a thing and don't know where you put the suitcases. You are now practicing the antithesis of living in the moment. You are ruining your lunch because you are caught up in yesterday and tomorrow.

The key to being happy (besides gratitude) is living in this very moment. Do not let your mind wander off. Stay in the present. There is a great book written by Jon Kabat-Zinn titled, <u>Mindfulness for Beginners</u>. If you would like help in learning this concept, this is a wonderful book. It will change your world. I highly recommend it. During retirement there are so many things to think about that often we just get overwhelmed. This book will help you to slow down and learn to tackle one subject at a time.

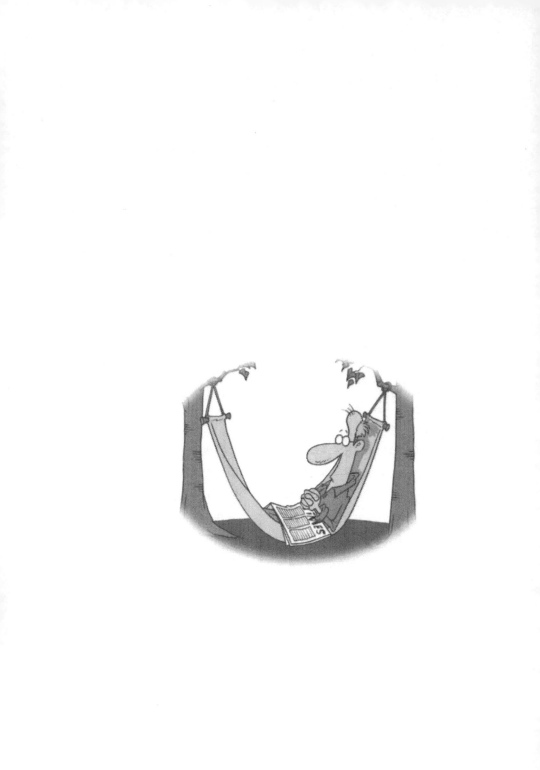

Adult Children

Many of you have raised your own children. Now most of your children are in their 40's, 50's, or 60's. It is great to have children that age because as time goes by they become more like adult friends than kids you changed diapers for years ago.

Sometimes adult children can put pressures on their retired parents that are uncomfortable, stressful, and downright rude. The most common concerns are borrowing money or living with their parents again or expecting a constant babysitter.

Let's tackle the money issue first. Everyone can have some bad luck. If you have a healthy nest egg of savings, perhaps you can loan your child some money. If your son/daughter borrows some money, be sure you have them sign an agreement of how and when they are going to pay back the loan. It can be so much a week, month, or year. If they are offended by doing this, don't loan them the money. It is quite simple. I remember my Dad loaned me money for my Master's degree. He even charged me interest on the loan. I paid back every penny.

Second, your children come to live with you. Perhaps it is because of a divorce, illness, or losing a job. Whatever the reason, again you should have them give you an expectation of how long they plan to stay. You also need to establish rules for your home. It is YOUR home and you make the guidelines. This is especially for younger adult children coming home. They often take advantage by staying out late, playing loud music, or having their current love stay overnight.

In other words, there are consequences to be paid for moving in with Mom and Dad. You didn't work hard for thirty or forty years to now babysit your adult children.

Grandchildren

Most folks love their grandchildren. I have met very few people who were not absolutely thrilled to have grandchildren. I still to this day remember my Grandmother's reaction when I would come to visit her. We lived in the same city, but when I would go to visit her, she would open the door, and act as if the King of England had just arrived. She would squeal with delight, throw her arms around me, and invite me in for cookies and milk.

My advice to grandparents is to love your grandkids and tell them how proud you are of them. As a teacher for 39 years, I heard so many parents tell me about the problems they were having with their teenagers. I also felt that if the parents and grandparents would simply say, " I am proud of you, " that many of these troubled kids would turn around. It is hard to act up and be irresponsible when your closest relatives are complimenting you.

However, I do have a cautionary remark here as well. Some adult children believe that grandparents are synonymous with the word babysitter. This is not fair. Of course, most young people rely on their parents to help babysit. It is often an economic necessity. Having said that, remember these are your retirement years and unless you want to be a full time babysitter, you have to make some ground rules with your adult kids. Yes, it may be awkward or tough, but you need your time alone for activities, festivities, and vacations. So just set some rules that everyone can agree on ahead of time.

Choose To Do The Things You Love

My friend Barbara Biancalana is semi - retired. She advocates doing the things she loves in this period of her life. It is an excellent concept. One of the things she loves is books. So she chooses to work a few hours in a book store. She loves being around books as she was an English major. Plus, she finds people who frequent book stores to be intellectually stimulating. Barbara simply likes the whole atmosphere of a book store.

She also likes children and has included them in her semi - retirement plans. It keeps her young at heart. She believes that kids radiate hope. Barbara likes to give back to the community. She is currently helping take care of an eleven year old girl whose mother recently committed suicide. Barbara is an excellent role model for giving service to others. She not only helps others, but it makes her feel like she is making a positive difference in her neighborhood.

Barbara states that being semi - retired is not about money. It is about feeling fulfilled as a human being. Barbara is the perfect example of making specific goals and plans for her older years. If you met her, you would see an enthusiastic and happy woman who is enjoying each and every day of her life.

Movies

There is nothing like seeing movies on the big screen. Going to a theater is a great outing for seniors. When you see a movie on the big screen there are no distractions like you have at home. There are no phones ringing, dogs barking, doorbells to be answered, or spouses asking questions.

Plus, there are discounts for retirees. You can see movies at most anytime and there is always a senior discount. Movies are expensive these days, but reasonable for older folks. Sometimes we get in a rut and just watch everything on television or the computer. Trust me when I say, you will love the big screen experience. It not only gets you out of the house, but you will enjoy the film experience much more.

So go see a movie this week!

Doctors

Choosing good doctors is important in your retirement years. The old adage is to pick a doctor who is younger than yourself so they don't retire on you. You need someone who knows your history. I personally like to become friends with my doctors. I feel like you get better service and it is also a comfort thing for me. I share everything that is going on in my life with them. It makes for a more balanced relationship between us. Instead of being the patient and doctor, we become two people who are friends concerned about my well- being.

I recently changed doctors. The first doctor was good, but was charging an arm and a leg for his services. Plus, he was too flip with his answers about my problems. He was a fun individual, but I wanted someone more serious. So I did switch to a new doctor who is calmer and more serious. He is an excellent listener and types everything into the computer as we talk. I believe being a good listener is the most important trait for a doctor to possess.

It is also important to schedule regular check-ups with your doctor. I know this sounds rather silly to say this at our age, but many folks, especially men, do not do this. It is imperative that you plan regular visits so illnesses can be avoided.

My partner, Steve, is a doctor. His advice is that the most important skill a doctor can have is to know when not to treat as much as when to treat. Many doctors over prescribe medicines and it screws up the whole body system

My friend Kevin is a retired surgeon. He feels a good doctor should be both compassionate and empathetic. Kevin says that doctors that can show compassion make the patient feel better and gives them confidence.

Volunteer Fatigue

Once we retire, many of us (myself included) volunteer. We volunteer for groups that we have a special fondness for like schools, charities, and health agencies.

It is wonderful to get involved in the community, giving your time and experience to others for the good of society. I have learned the hard way that sometimes you can get so involved with your local volunteer activities that you feel you are working full time. Most organizations have a fairly significant turn- over rate and that requires long term volunteers to pick up the slack. If you are a person that constantly says, " yes, " you will discover that your free retirement time is evaporating. This will bring on resentment and you don't want that during your retirement.

So map out ahead of time how much of your valuable time you want to devote to your special organization. If you carefully plan ahead, you can avoid the pitfalls of volunteer fatigue.

Get Plenty of Rest

My friend, Dorothy Young is a wonderful artist. She says that as we age there seem to be more appointments like the eye doctor, the dentist, getting hearing aids, having the car serviced, and helping friends and neighbors with their appointments. The list becomes endless so she believes rest is very important.

Another point Dorothy made was setting a routine and time for your hobby. She said to set a time for your hobby like it was an important meeting. If you don't make the time, you will not do it. Dorothy suggested that if you don't have a hobby, find one.

Volunteering was high on her list as well, but again making sure you set a time for it. She believes it keeps you young. Again, Dorothy states that you will be busier than you ever dreamed of, so it is important to make sure you take care of yourself by getting lots of rest.

Variety in Retirement

Carole Nelson has been retired for fifteen years. She loves to have a variety of activities during her retirement years.

Carole joined a Book Club where she met new friends and enjoyed their opinions on various books that the club read. She came to the realization that she can never read all the books she wants to so Carole is not even going to try!

She loves being able to go on vacations with her older children and granddaughters. Since she is retired, she can go most anytime. Carole is from the Midwest so she would ask her family, " would you like white snow or white sand?" Since white sand usually wins out, Cancun has been a favorite escape for years.

Golfing has been a wonderful activity in her life. She joined a women's group and they enjoy other activities during the year besides golf. She reminds us that health is important and you have to take care of yourself. I think this sentence of hers is so powerful, " As long as you have your health, anything is possible, but you've got to take care of yourself or it doesn't matter how high you've piled your retirement fund. " Carole is so right.

Carole is another person who joined the Osher Lifelong Learning Institute. Her philosophy is that, " you should try to learn something new every day and flex your brain by using it." I agree with that idea.

Carole volunteers within her community. She joined a church group which is making baby blankets that they distribute during the year. She has also been active in her church with the ESL (English as a Second Language) program. As Carole states, " If you have special talents to share with others, retirement is a great time to give back." The bottom line is that Carole is proactive in her retirement with a variety of activities. She is a great role model.

Plan A Special Activity

My friend Jim Davis wrote the following sage wisdom:

What advice could I give you for retirement? Of course, everyone will tell you to plan, plan, and plan. There are the usual plans to make...financial, where to live, and those kinds of things.

I did all those things, but there was one thing I overlooked. As I look back, I was fortunate enough to stumble through that one thing. That was to be certain that I planned on a way to stay active. Have a reason to get up every morning, and have some sort of routine.

After many years in the corporate world, I decided to become a massage therapist. I loved the change and did well. Upon retirement, it turned out to be a fortunate choice. It meant that I could set my own schedule, do something that I love and most of all, avoid boredom. When I have a slow week, I become aware of how much I need activity in my life.

So regardless of what it is – plan for some type of activity in retirement that will give you that sense of being alive. You may have to ponder this somewhat to discover what it is. Time spent discovering this special activity is time well spent.

Retirement Choices

My friend Sue Robinson Neeb shared her thoughts about retirement:

Retirement – a sometimes scary word to some people.

As you reach retirement, the choices are endless as to how you choose to spend the rest of your life. Like the past life you have already lived – it is all about the choices you make.

You can choose to look forward to having more time for the things you enjoy. Or, better yet, find new things to interest you. You can spend more time with the people who make you laugh. You can take time to learn a new skill or hobby.

The people who truly enjoy retirement are the ones who look forward to each day and each new experience or person that may come into their life. Again, it is all about the choices you make.

You may experience some losses as people and places fade away from your life, but it is all part of the living and maturing process. Sometimes it may make you sad to see things change. You need to accept those changes as the natural life progression.

It is a great time to reflect on things you have done that bring a smile to your face and perhaps do them again. It may be better " the second time around " – who knows until you try it?

Please spend your time and energy on things that bring you joy and fulfillment – don't go to the end of your life and have to say, " I wish I had….."

Attitude

Dale Carnegie said, " Remember, happiness doesn't depend upon who you are or what you have, it depends solely upon what you think."

This thought is important to remember during your retirement years. As we age, it is easy and convenient to talk about the way things used to be when we were younger and growing up. Sure things have changed, they always do. Yes, some of the changes are not good, but many, such as the advances in medicine and technology are awesome. Computers and Smart phones were not around when we were growing up, but now they are everywhere. They have made the world more connected and advanced.

When you get up in the morning, stop for a few minutes and think about your attitude for the day. If it is in negative territory, try to turn it around. When I begin to throw a pity party for myself, I always think of the folks that endured the Holocaust. If some of them could survive the horrific conditions the Nazis put them through, then I can find a solution to my small little problems. Hitler's Germany put Jews, Catholics, Gays, Jehovah Witnesses, Unionists, and Political people into the concentration camps. I have read books about the survivors of the camps. Most attribute their survival to their attitudes and a bit of luck. Attitude is everything in life.

" I keep my ideals, because in spite of everything, I still believe that people are really good at heart." Anne Frank

If Anne Frank could have such an upbeat attitude during the nightmare of World War II, we can most certainly have the same during our retirement years.

Driving

Being independent during your retirement years is a priority for most people. This means being able to get into your car and drive to any place you want to visit. It is most important to pay attention to everything while you drive. As we age, it is more difficult to focus our attention. Driving requires your full attention.

For instance, I rear ended a woman this last year because I thought the light had changed and pressed the gas pedal. I only hit her at 3 mph, but it ended up being an expensive experience for my car insurance company. The woman had only a scratch on her bumper, but she soaked the company for money. She claimed that she had neck and back injuries. Of course, she couldn't see a doctor for a week as she was going on vacation. Gee, she could go on vacation, but not to the doctor? Anyhow, the whole thing was bogus! The bottom line is she received $5,000 from my insurance company plus my $500 deductible. It was pure fraud.

So be alert and careful when driving. Plus, if you have been drinking, let someone else drive. Getting a DUI during retirement is expensive, frustrating, and very inconvenient.

Stop Complaining

Today I was at my printer's office. There was a fireman talking with the printer. He talked about his retired friend that he took to the casino. They had dinner, saw a show, and did valet parking. The fireman said this friend complained about everything. He even complained about paying for valet parking. He told his fireman friend he had never seen so many fat people, but there he was standing in the parking lot waiting for someone to drive the car up to him!

The fireman was telling us this whole story as he made the observation that people can't just retire without a plan. They need to do something to occupy their time. Like he said, " many retirees just become complainers and food critics." There is certainly more to life than being critical of everything. Always look for the positive if you want to enjoy your later years.

Bocci Ball

Bocci Ball is a popular activity with retirees these days. They have many players in 55+ developments. It is not difficult to play even if you have arthritis. You simply bend down to roll the ball. Many places have team competitions so it is a great place to meet new people. My cousin, Sharon and her husband Ron play on a team. They absolutely love it.

Another activity they suggest is Shuffleboard. It requires about the same amount of energy as Bocci Ball so it is quite popular, too. If you are not into golf, Bocci Ball and Shuffleboard might be two great alternatives for fun and exercise.

Shoes

This might sound like a humorous topic, but it is quite serious. When we retire, we think of relaxation. So this means not having to wear shoes or at a minimum just wearing flip flops or sandals. This is fine if you live in a warm climate and are trying to stay cool. Having just said that, it isn't so good if you have bad feet.

During your retirement years, you should wear arch supports or orthotics to help support your arches and feet. I can tell you from my own experience that it is important to wear proper shoes. I have very flat feet and when I wear my flip flops too much, my feet really ache. I have been getting a weekly foot massage of late as my feet are hurting that much.

So take care of your feet.....retirement will not be fun if walking is always painful.

Stop to Smell the Flowers and Everything Else

My Dad always wonders why everyone is in such a hurry. Now that you are retired, you can slow down.

I notice the mountains that surround the valley here in Palm Springs. I am constantly awed by their beauty. They change hues all day long. I notice people's lawns and homes. I take time to pet dogs whose owners have them on leashes during morning walks. I talk to people in the grocery store, shopping mall, or on the street. I make a conscious effort to enjoy the world around me.

Some of us will not be able to travel far during retirement, but you can always appreciate what you have around your home and city. There are always things to be grateful for in every city, town, and state. In other words, don't be in such a rush to get everything done. Relax a bit more as you don't have an office deadline anymore! Take time to "smell the flowers."

AARP

AARP is a great organization to belong to during your retirement years. It is a great resource for medical tips, travel discounts, volunteer ideas, and just about everything else. Plus, by joining the organization you get discounts for all kinds of things from insurance premiums to large department store deals. Plus, they advocate for the political things that matter most to seniors.

The AARP magazine is a must. It really addresses so many things about aging and retirement. I always learn something new after reading it. Inside the magazine are hints of every kind and variety. These suggestions can be about health, home repair, cruise specials, or tips for being a grandmother or grandfather. It is all good!

So become a member of AARP. You will never regret it!

The Bottom Line Personal

The Bottom Line is the other magazine I recommend for your retirement years. It is a small publication that comes every month. It includes information and tips for making stock investments, wills, and bond purchases. It also has information about health and health products. It has a whole variety of topics.

Here are some recent article titles:

Best foreign stock bargains; Natural Rx for migraines; Top large-cap growth funds; Beware : the fake survey call; Better way to plan for retirement health expenses; Clean where it is hard to clean; the one minute workout; 12 cool things you can do with your smart phone; and foods that help you sleep.

This magazine is great and generally it is less than 20 pages. So it is a quick and easy read. I have no hidden agenda with this publication other than the fact I love it. Google it online and find out for yourself. They also publish another magazine called, <u>Bottom Line Health</u>. It is equally informative. Try subscribing to them for a year.....I think you will thank me.

Join a Gym

I live in the California desert so weather is good all year long. I can do my outdoor walking every day of the year. Many people live in colder climates so joining a gym is a great idea. It is always helpful if you can go with a partner or group of friends as they keep you motivated.

It is important to read the fine print when joining a gym. Sometimes they make you pay for a full year or have you pay a penalty for deciding to stop earlier than your contract.

The gym has so many advantages. You can go to the gym any time of the day or night. You have the options of many kinds of weight training and cardio machines. Plus, many gyms have swimming pools and sauna's. They also have classes on nutrition, weight loss, and healthy living. So it is all good.

The most important thing is getting into the habit of going to the gym. I have heard through the years that we form habits in 21 days. Perhaps if you go to the gym for that same time, you will become a life time member.

Dinner Clubs

We all enjoy eating. It seems that dinners are the most significant meals of the day. Folks go out for a fancy dinner to celebrate birthdays, anniversaries, and a host of other events. During the working years, many people didn't have time or the energy to cook a special dinner at home. So why not create a dinner club now?

Some of my friends have started these clubs where they get perhaps four to five couples to participate. Each couple selects a month and they prepare a special dinner for the other members of the club. It is a wonderful way to explore new recipes and tastes. It not only gives people a new way to socialize, but it also tweaks your brain to try something new. It even sharpens one's cognitive skills to read and research new recipes.

The key to making dinner clubs successful is to make them fun and not a chore. So some clubs meet every other month. Some do potluck so it isn't so much work for the hosts. All members have to agree on how many people they feel comfortable serving. It is simply another fun activity to consider during retirement. Bon Appetite!

Dating Online

Many people who reach retirement age are divorced, widowed, or single. Now that work is no longer mandatory, it presents more opportunities to find a friend or future spouse.

Many of my friends now use online dating services. Many of us at this age think it is not cool to do such a thing, but it is a new way of meeting people. In the old days we would meet people through work, parties, family gatherings, or bars. Now you can hook up with people by the touch of your computer keys.

As a matter of fact, two of my favorite people met each other online and got married. So I do think it is a useful tool for meeting future partners or spouses.

My advice would be this.....do not believe everything a person writes on their profile page. Many people pad the truth. The other suggestion would be to meet at a restaurant or coffee bar for your first meeting. A bar or nightclub just doesn't cut it. Booze can impair your judgment. So I would have a sober first date.

Again, I know it is uncomfortable for some people to use their computers for a dating service, but it has worked for thousands, if not millions of people around the world. Best of luck!

Join AAA

A few years ago, we saw Liza Minnelli on stage at the Morongo Casino in Cabazon, California. Cabazon is about 20 minutes from Palm Springs. It was a terrific concert. We were in great moods driving home. I turned off Interstate 10 and on to Highway 111 which goes into Palm Springs. The highway runs through remote desert with nothing but rocks and the mountains to the west. It was black as spades that night in the desert. All of a sudden, we heard a big bang. My right rear tire had exploded. I pulled over to the shoulder onto the sand.

It was scary being all alone out on that very dark road. All we could think about were coyotes and mountain lions patrolling the area. Plus, we were worried about gang bangers trying to help us out and then robbing us or worse. Lucky for us, I had my cell phone. I called Triple A and they were there in 20 minutes. You can't imagine the relief to see the Triple A truck drive up with its lights flashing. The young man immediately changed the flat tire. He even waited for us to get back on the highway before driving away himself.

Triple A is one of the best organizations around. They are there when you need their help. Once, my battery went dead in a parking lot. I called Triple A. Again they were there in a few minutes. He looked at my battery and noticed I still had four months on my warranty. Since I had purchased it from Triple A, I got a new battery for free. So I truly believe that Triple A is a must for all retirees.

Tim Cook's Advice

Apple CEO Tim Cook delivered a graduation address at George Washington University in 2015. He told the graduating seniors not to "spend their lives on the sidelines." His message was originally directed to these young graduates, but I find his words just as meaningful for retirees. Just because you retire doesn't mean you stop making a difference in the world. Now that many of us have the money and time, we can still make changes in our community, state, nation, and the world.

Tim said, " there are problems that need to be solved, injustices that need to be ended. People that are still being persecuted. Diseases are still in need of a cure. No matter what you do next, the world needs your energy and passion to progress. History rarely yields to one person, but think and never forget what happens when it does. That can be you. That should be you. That must be you."

So think about using some of your retirement time to make a difference in a cause that is important to you. Spread your passion around and make a positive contribution to society. You will feel great and others will be better off because you made the world a better place.

Mary Barbara Lemke

My friend Mary Barbara turned 100 on May 28, 2015. She is an advocate for working as long as possible. She finally retired from a job as a secretary at an avocado ranch in Southern California. How old was she when she retired? She was 76. She probably would have stayed longer at her job, but she needed to take care of family members who were ill.

Her key advice for retirement is to stay busy with projects. They could be simple things like cleaning out drawers and throwing out stuff you don't need or use any longer. Mary Barbara also has fun goals like reading lots of books. She has read over 800 books while being retired.

She is also a scrapbook person. She has made many scrapbooks that were not just full of photos, but articles and cards people would send her. She makes greeting cards. Mary Barbara is a prolific letter writer. She writes the most wonderful letters on yellow legal sized paper using both sides. When I receive a letter from her, it is like getting a bar of gold. I could sit down and read her words for hours.

She is active in her beautiful mobile home park. She attends the dinners and events at the clubhouse. Plus, she walks around the park every day of the year. Walking is very important to her.

My point is that Mary Barbara never just sits and looks at the television. She stays active and makes projects for each day. Although she has not traveled the world, she is one of the wisest people I have ever met. I believe she has made it to the century mark because she stays active and involved in life. She is a role model for all retired people.

My Dad's Advice

I asked my 89 year old Dad what suggestions he would give to people who are facing retirement. Here are his words:

" Several weeks ago, my son asked me to write a short paragraph on retirement. Naturally, it required a profound statement of great insight since my son is a learned teacher of great repute. But that great burst of light has yet to appear! My retirement so far is going on 25 years and the few things that come to mind are keep active, do all the things you can as often as you can as it is nourishment for the body, mind, and soul. And, appreciate the good you see in your friends and family."

Write Your Memoirs

My friend Michael Pettit suggested that when you retire, you can do all those things you wanted to do, but couldn't do when you were working. The things you gave up can now be revived.

One activity would be to write your memoirs. Michael had a tough childhood, filled with rejection and challenges. He enrolled in a class about how to write your autobiography and is writing a book about those early childhood years in hopes that it will help others who might be in the same situation. He succeeded where others might have given up. He ended up being a talented court reporter and was a successful realtor. Today he is a very contented man comfortable with his personal and professional life.

Writing your memoirs is a way to help others remember your life and learn from it. Plus, it is a project that lets you review your life. Most folks find it deeply satisfying to write their stories. So start writing!

Counseling and Therapy

As we get older people expect us to know all of the answers about life. Guess what? We don't know all of the solutions to the many problems in life.

I believe everyone benefits from going to a therapist or a counselor. You need to pick the right counselor or therapist for you. I went to a counselor for years whose name was Betty. She was very nurturing and I always felt so much better after I left her office. I had been fearful of moving from teaching at the middle school to the high school. She helped me through my fears and I ultimately transferred to the high school.

I will never forget a student coming up to me in the hall the first day of school in September. He had been a student of mine at the middle school. He said, " Are you here at the high school for good? " I answered," yes." The student responded with, " You should have moved over here ten years ago. " Here I had worried about going to the high school and one of my former students was validating my move. However, I probably would not have moved had it not been for my wonderful counselor.

I have gone to therapy since I retired as I had other issues I wanted to discuss with a third party. I had issues about my partner's health, friends, and family. The counselor helped me with all of these issues. So now that you are retired, you have more time to fit counseling into your schedule. I will be blunt. Most folks have issues, but many people will go to their graves without coming to terms with these problems. So my suggestion is to go to counseling while you are retired. Get any stressful issues out of the way and make retirement more relaxing.

Retirement – Why Not Phase Into It?

Many folks are unsure about retirement. My suggestion is to retire the way I did. Here is my short story that worked well for me. I retired in phases.

Phase 1 - I retired from my full time teaching job up in Portland, Oregon. I had taught for 30 years and was ready to finally slow down after years of making lessons, facing report card deadlines, dealing with computer problems, and planning parent conferences.

Phase 2 – When I moved to the desert, I decided to teach part time. I taught two classes of history for the next nine years. It gave me something to do, but the work load was cut in half. I had plenty of time for other activities. Plus, I was at a private school where there were not a lot of state mandates on what we could or could not do. So it was easy street after public school teaching.

Phase 3 – After teaching part time for almost ten years, I actually retired. It was a smooth transition for me. So I did the full time, then the part time, and then retired permanently.

Perhaps you can do something like I did if you have reservations about an abrupt retirement. It really worked well for me as I was totally ready to retire. I had activities, friends, and groups that were in place when I retired.

The Bathroom Conversation

How sexy is it to talk about our bathroom habits during retirement???
Well, most of us would agree they are far from sexy. However, for a
good retirement you need healthy bathroom habits. When we were all
working, we had a routine. After you quit working, your hours change
and somethings get out of whack.

I discovered a great product called MetaMucil. It has been around for
years. It provides you lots of fiber and it comes in a tasty orange flavor.
Trust me, after years of problems, this product keeps me regular and
on schedule. It is the best piece of advice I can give to my family,
friends, and readers of this book.

If you have never had any bowel problems by now, you are lucky.
However, many people develop them in their later years. The last
thing you want during retirement is bathroom challenges. I had a
horrific experience in London years ago. I know that incident would
have never happened if I had been taking my daily dose of MetaMucil.

So try this product or a similar one. It will make retirement much more
pleasant as you will feel better physically and have no worries about
the bathroom when you are out traveling, visiting friends, or just going
to the grocery store.

Taking Pictures

My motto is that you can never take too many photographs. This is especially true now in the digital age where you can delete pictures instantly if you don't like them or add five new ones to your picture folders on the computer.

I have been a photo-holic for years. It has served me well. I framed pictures, I made scrapbooks, I made posters, I made coffee cups, I made coasters, and many other creative things using my photos. People love remembering the fun times of the past.

I also have always had a large wall with many, many frames of photographs. People love to look at them when they come to our house. Sure, some people have died or moved on, but everyone is still smiling. It leaves people with good feelings inside.

Now that you are retiring, you can have lots of fun with photographs. It is so easy these days and there are so many more things you can do with a digital camera. Don't stop taking pictures because you are getting older. They will always be special to so many people and especially to you.

Retirement Advice from Two Teachers

My friends Dennis and Mary Rogers live in Issaquah, Washington which is a suburb of Seattle. They have both taught for over thirty years. Both Mary and Dennis were outstanding teachers. I asked them to share a little advice about retirement. Here are their thoughts:

Dennis:

" One of the best things Mary and I did was to head to Glacier and Yellowstone National Parks when school opened in September. It was a wonderful transition to retirement. It helped me ignore school starting without me and then realizing the children could learn without my help. Sometimes it is a good idea to get out of town."

Mary:

" Hold on to some of the joy that you had in your career. For me, that has been substituting after teaching full time for 35 years. I still see students and hopefully have a positive impact in their lives and I'm blessed to spend more time with the wonderful people I worked with for so long."

I really think their comments are perceptive about retirement. They are excellent thoughts for all retirees to digest.

Retirement vs Reconsideration

My good friend Rich Callen submitted this thoughtful piece about retirement. Enjoy reading Rich's perceptive ideas:

Having retired from architecture and design at the age of 65 following forty-plus years of active employment in the profession of working on international hotel/resort projects, I was ready to make long envisioned changes in my life. This included moving to Mexico, partnering with two longtime friends, and buying a triplex in Puerto Vallarta. Our intention was to convert the property into three separate living spaces. However, after having purchased a property in Puerto Vallarta and dealing with upgrade and renovation options, I realized my feelings for a person I met and remained in touch with in Los Angeles were far more serious than I had admitted to myself.

We opted to rent out the property in Mexico, selling it a couple years later and I returned to Southern California. I committed to a solid relationship with my partner taking up residence in Ventura seven years ago. I am now being lured back into the design industry via a consulting position with a former business partner in Los Cabos, BCS, Mexico. I now must admit to the fact that I loved my years in the architecture/design industry. Deep down, I missed the satisfaction of following the vision-thru-development of projects around the globe for over four decades.

During the past seven years, I filled my days with volunteer projects, tutoring elementary school children and shopping for those residents in our retired residential community who were no longer able to drive themselves to markets or doctor appointments. I'm determined to combine my current design-related goals with the commitment to my long - running volunteer services in my community. Thanks to Skype

communications, phone, e-mail, and FedEx, I've been able to work from my home scheduling my own hours and still maintaining a semi-limited volunteer schedule.

Here's my advice to those seriously considering retirement from any profession they truly enjoy and are not concerned about the future financial impact relating to maintaining a comfortable lifestyle, whether funded by Social Security, investment income, or pensions: Take plenty of time to think through the actual reality of your decision and how it will affect your future well- being as you enter the proverbial " Golden Years " of your life. In other words, do what you love for as long as you're physically and mentally able to do so.

Richard Callen

Hospital Visits

This book is about how to have a fulfilling retirement, but let's face reality. We are at the age where friends and family are going to have major medical issues. Many of those challenges will require surgeries and time in hospitals.

Since you will be retired, you may feel expected to visit your friends, co-workers, or family in the hospital. Please WAIT. Many patients DO NOT want to see visitors when they are in the hospital. They have not showered, washed their hair, shaved, or brushed their teeth and they just plain don't feel good.

Most patients will be in some sort of pain or adverse medical state. They often will not feel like trying to make conversation with others. So it is most important that you phone or text either the patient or a family member to see if the patient wants company. You will save yourself from an embarrassing situation by doing this small act. Plus, you will probably find out later that the patient appreciated not having a visitor until they were feeling better.

Chiropractic Care Can Improve Your Retirement

As you get older, the discs between your vertebra become thinner because they lose some of the fluid inside them. As you may have noticed, we all get a little shorter in old age and this is the reason why. Vertebral discs are like a sponge. By gently tractioning the vertebra apart, the traction acts to pull more fluid from the body to thicken the discs. Even a couple of millimeters of thickening can make the difference between a painful back and a non – painful one.

The most difficult part of this whole process is finding the right Chiropractor and the right technique for you to bring you help. I always advise patients to ask their friends about their experiences to find the right doctor. This is very true of finding the right Medical doctors, as well. Never be afraid to try a new doctor if the one you have is not helping you. There are many good Chiropractors and Medical doctors everywhere, but there are also many who are not so good. Keep looking, you will find someone you connect with and you will know it.

Chiropractors, like their medical counter parts can provide an enormous amount of good information about lifestyle changes, exercises, and diet as well as many other topics. They can also be a resource for community services and activities that can add great value to your quality of life.

Lastly, never underestimate the value of human touch to your health and well – being. Just having a Chiropractor rub a sore spot, massage a muscle or hold your hand can bring great comfort. Chiropractors spend eight years of higher education learning all about the human body and

how to help it without the use of drugs and surgery. Many people have a great misconception of our education. It is far more extensive than you may know.

I wish you good health and happiness in your retirement years.

Steve Oliver, DC

Don't Become A Victim of Rustout

Richard Leider and Steve Buchhoz wrote, The Rustout Syndrome. According to these two authors, " Rustout is the slow death that follows when we stop making the choices that keep life alive. It's the feeling of numbness that comes from always taking the safe way, never accepting new challenges, continually surrendering to the day-to-day routine." Basically they are saying that people often go into a survival mode rather than a thriving place in their lives.

This is an easy cavern to fall into during the retirement years. I see it with many people I personally know. They have a routine and damn, nothing is going to change it. They are comfortable with it and nothing is going to interfere with it. Perhaps this is fine, if they are happy with their day to day to habits. However, if they are depressed, lonely, and restless, then they should consider changing their days and weeks.

So if you are suffering from " rustout " go ahead and make some changes in your retirement life. Explore something new.

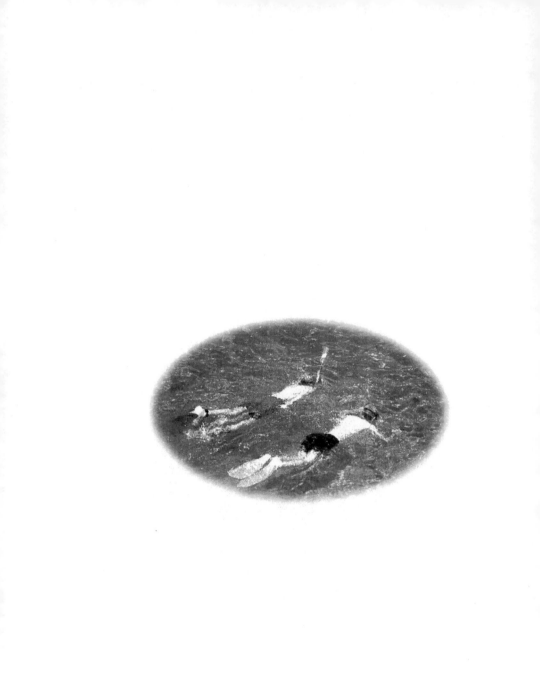

Chair Disease

There has been a lot written lately about how much time we spend sitting in our favorite chairs. We sit too many hours in front of our computers and televisions. Then we go to the kitchen table and sit there for too many hours. This is not a good thing. Experts are now calling it ' Chair Disease' because it causes health problems. It has been associated with early death, diabetes, and heart disease.

Yes, we all do a lot of sitting that is necessary, but the goal should be to take breaks from sitting. Time yourself to get up out of your chair every 20 minutes and walk around the house or take a short walk around the block. Just get the circulation going again in your body. Many of us have work on our computers, but sitting for hours on end is not healthy. If the phone rings, walk around the house while you are talking.

Television programs are filled with commercials. So when commercials come on start walking around the house or do some quick exercises like jumping jacks to get movement in your body. As you know, there are lots of commercials so you will be able to get lots of exercise if you get up for every commercial.

Don't become a victim of ' Chair Disease ' . If you are confined most of the time to a chair, wiggle your toes, try to stretch, and lift your legs a bit. Every movement helps.

Never Give Up Your Dream

The Cal State graduation class 2015 had a unique graduate this year. His name is Bill McCloud. He is the oldest student to graduate from Cal State, San Bernardino in Palm Desert. Bill is 85 years old. He has always wanted to get his teaching certificate and he finally realized his dream in 2015. Not only has this been his goal to receive his degree, but now he wants to actually teach students.

He feels he has something to offer young people and plans to hunt for a part time job. The point is that this man never said, " I am too old, I don't have time, or I am not smart enough." He set his goal and never took his eyes off it. I think he is an excellent role model for all retirees. Age is a just a number……don't let it prevent you from fulfilling any of your dreams.

A Delicate Balance

My first school secretary was a funny and warm lady named Maxine. She and her husband Duane had a perfect marriage. They took lots of trips and always were very social. Then Duane retired early. Almost immediately, the dynamics of their marriage changed and not in a positive way.

One day Maxine came to school and said, " I am about ready to kill Duane. " Apparently, Duane had no hobbies or plans for his retirement. So when Maxine would arrive home from work, he followed her around the house like a little puppy dog. Worse yet, when she was ironing or cooking he would give her tips on how to do each chore better. The bottom line was Duane was driving her crazy because he had nothing to do with his time.

I have found this to be quite true with many couples. When one retires before the other, they don't plan on how to spend their days. You must have a plan for activities or you will drive your spouse nuts.

Equally true is when you both retire at the same time. You need some activities separate from your spouse. In other words, give each other some space.

As Times Change, Time Changes

This very original and clever contribution was written by my good friend Doug Halm. Enjoy!

If you're worried about how you'll spend your time once you've retired, worry not. Even if you don't take the excellent advice of others to spend more time volunteering, exercising, taking courses or rediscovering past hobbies, you'll still find yourself running out of time. How's that possible? The answer is simple: as you comfortably settle into retirement, your internal clock begins to reset itself. The *relativity of time* changes. I know that sounds incredible so I have illustrated this phenomenon with a simple comparison of my morning routine before and after retirement.

Before: My alarm would go off at 6:30 a.m. I'd reluctantly crawl out of bed and stumble outside to get the newspaper. I'd peruse it quickly – no time for more than that. I'd usually grab a muffin and gulp down a cup of coffee while multi – tasking through my e-mails. Next I'd shave and then hop into the shower. I'd dress by grabbing any shirt that appeared to be ironed, taking a second to also ensure my socks matched. Sometimes they didn't. Then I'd rush out the door to get to work on time – I always seemed to be running late!

Duration: 1 hour and 5 minutes

After: My alarm goes off at 6:30 a.m. I press ' snooze ' and continue to press it until it's 8:00 a.m., a more civilized time to arise. I retrieve the newspaper from my driveway, sometimes lingering to kibitz with my retired neighbor. (It's our opportunity to solve the world's problems.) Back in bed, I read every newspaper article that is of even minimal interest. I check for sales at Target or

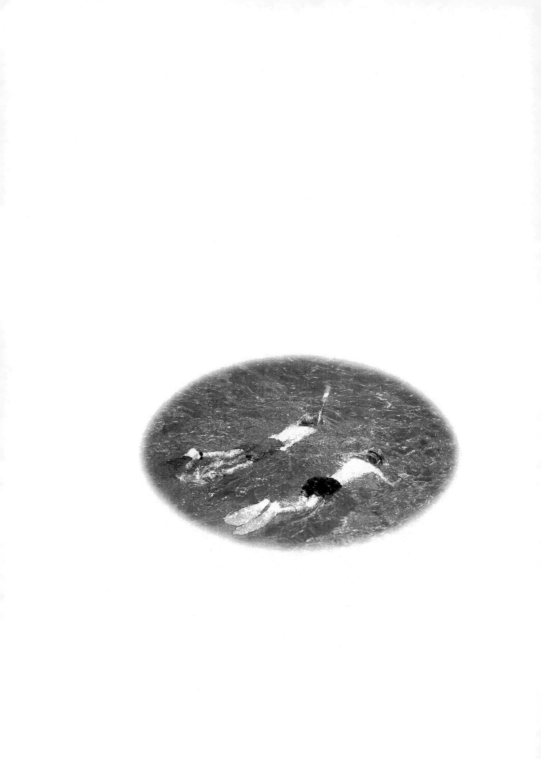

Kohls's and tear out any Bed, Bath & Beyond coupons (save them – they actually don't expire). By the way, it's a myth to think that you won't be buying more stuff once you've retired. You actually buy more because you've got lots of time to think about things you want....and lots of time to buy them! I enjoy two, maybe three leisurely cups of coffee now. I read all of my e-mails, even ones from Nigeria. I also take time to e-mail friends, arranging future coffee dates and cocktail parties.

I then plan breakfast. Will it be a cheese omelet or banana pancakes today? I check online for a scrumptious Paula Deen recipe. (I love my breakfasts.) My showers are often preceded by a soak in the Jacuzzi which I find quite relaxing. I now have more clothing options since everything in my closet is ironed and arranged by hue, not unlike a *California Closets* ad. If I have a loose button, I fix it. Sometimes I have another cup of coffee to get me through this arduous task.

I watch CNN...or even FOX News, if I'm curious what the enemy is up to. Often I take time to program my DVR for the entire week just so I don't miss anything. If I feel like it, I might re-alphabetize my spice drawer, detail my car or mop the garage floor. I find that mornings are also a good time schedule doctors' appointments (we're not getting any younger) or plan my weekly Costco run. Am I down to nine rolls of TP already?

Sometimes I run errands – pick up my Rx refills, take the dog to Petco or do some shopping for myself. Since my retirement account is not what I had hoped it would be, I only buy stuff that's at least 30% off. Usually it's about noon by this time so I head home to make lunch. I am determined to create the ultimate ham and gruyere sandwich with my new panini. That takes a lot of practice and, quite frankly, can be a bit exhausting. Fortunately, that's what afternoon naps are for (I really

look forward to my nap time).   As you can see, my morning routine now sucks up more time than a Hoover upright. What used to take an hour has morphed into five. In fact, I've run out of time again just by telling you this little story.

Duration: 4 hours and 55 minutes

Thoughts on Retirement

After a 30 year legal career, with the last 12 years managing a large office of lawyers and legal assistants, I decided to retire at the age of 59. That decision was made 7 years ago and one that I certainly do not regret. I would like to briefly set out what I feel are practical and useful topics for anyone contemplating retirement

1) Health

Without a doubt, this is the single most important aspect of your retirement. We all take it for granted (until we really get sick) but without your health, both mental and physical, it is difficult to enjoy all the other elements of retirement. There are many aspects of our health that we cannot control. However, you should try and control what you can. To maintain mental health, you need to use your mind. That can be achieved by playing games, doing crosswords, learning another language or skill, etc. To maintain physical health, good nutrition and exercise are key. For good nutrition, it is necessary to eat the right foods and the right amount of food. For physical exercise, this may be playing a sport, working out at the gym or simply going for a walk.

2) Time (or what to do with it)

When you are retired, you have a new challenge. All of the time you spent working is now available to do whatever you want to do. Make no mistake, that is a lot of hours to fill. To fully enjoy your new life, you need to become an expert at planning and decision making. Before you retire, it is wise to know what you would like to do during retirement and recognize that you cannot just " put your feet up and relax." As most activities in life do not just spontaneously happen, you need to decide what you want to do and then go and do whatever that

may be. The list to choose from is endless and depends on your own life experience. Some of your choices may include the following- traveling, playing sports, reading the daily news, doing e-mail or interacting on social media, taking educational courses, volunteering, gardening or working on your house or condo, finding hobbies, having coffee, lunches, or dinner with friends, going to shows, shopping, cooking, playing a musical instrument, reading – whatever you personally enjoy. Doing activities that you like to do will make your retirement more enjoyable and fulfilling.

3) Friendships –(family, work and personal)

Most people need to interact with others – it makes life less solitary. After retirement, you will probably find that your personal relationships consist of family, work friends, personal friends and what I will call activity friends. The latter are friends you make through whatever activities you do in retirement. Your family situation will dictate how often you have family dinners or gatherings. You will keep your closer work friends. However, many work friendships may fade away as you are now retired and your work friends must still go to work. You will keep your personal friends, but it helps to reach out to them and make plans to see each other. An interesting aspect of retirement is that you will undoubtedly make new friends through whatever activities you choose during your retirement. For example, you may join a bridge club, tennis club or walking group. Any activity you do with others will result in new friendships that will enrich your life.

4) State of mind

If you are enjoying your retirement then you will have reached a state of mind where you are very content or pleased with how your retirement is unfolding. Another way of describing this is to say that you are feeling happy with your life. If your retirement does not go as you had hoped, then you should make whatever changes you think are required so that you do feel very satisfied with your life.

Hopefully, the thoughts set out above will guide you towards enjoying your retirement. Although not for everyone, for most of us retirement is a welcome and rewarding part of our life.

By Bill McClintock

Final Thoughts on Retirement

The purpose of this book on retirement was to give you some ideas, thoughts, and insights into your retirement years. How you spend them is purely up to you, but I hope you got some new ideas and perspectives about how to have a fulfilling retirement.

Jane Fonda recently discussed her new series <u>Grace and Frankie</u>, "We dispel the traditional view of aging. You're born, you peak at midlife, then you decline into age. That's an arc. For most people, life is more of an upward evolution. Research suggests that older people feel happier and less hostile, and that life gets easier. "

Her co-star, Lily Tomlin, added this comment, " Gee, I never thought this day would come. But you know what? I'm 75, and it's not bad."

So whatever your station in life, may you have a healthy and happy retirement. It is all up to you!

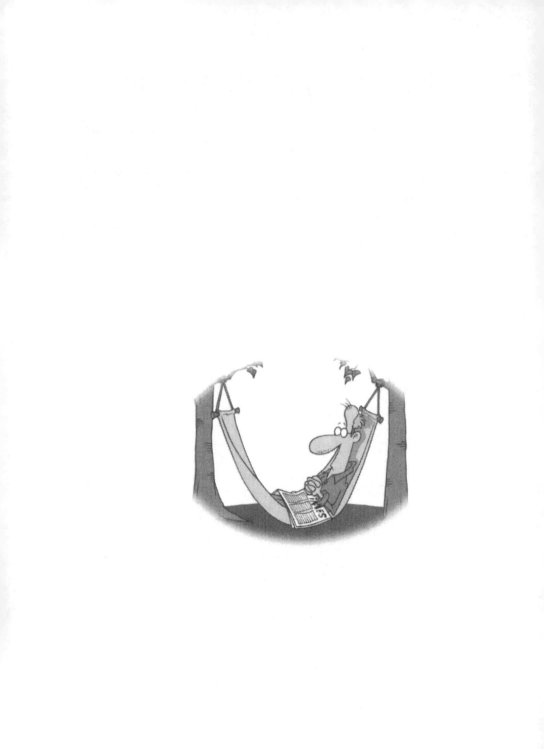

Retirement Quotations to Ponder

I've been attending lots of seminars in my retirement. They're called naps."   Merri Brownworth

" Retirement: It's nice to get out of the rat race, but you have to learn to get along with less cheese. "   Gene Perret

" I'm retired – goodbye tension, hello pension! "   Unknown

" Retirement can be a great joy if you can figure out how to spend time without spending money."   Unknown

" Don't simply retire *from* something; have something to retire *to*."

Harry Emerson

" Retire from work, but not from life."   M.K. Soni

" Retirement at sixty-five is ridiculous. When I was sixty-five I still had pimples."   George Burns

" First you forget names; then you forget faces; then you forget to zip up your fly; and then you forget to zip up your fly."   Branch Rickey

" Retirement kills more people than hard work ever did."
Malcolm Forbes

" Retirement: That's when you return from work one day and say, Hi, Honey, I'm home – forever."   Gene Perret

" I need to retire from retirement."   Sandra Day O'Connor

" Even when I retired, there was a part of me that didn't want to retire. But once you decide it's time to move on then you have to stick with it."   John Elway

" You can retire from a job, but don't ever retire from making contributions to life. "   Stephen Covey

" Sooner or later I'm going to die, but I am not going to retire."
Margaret Mead

" I keep going because if you stop, you stop. Why retire? Inspire."
Mickey Rooney

" I will not retire while I've still got my legs and my make-up box."
Bette Davis

" Writers don't retire. I will always be a writer."   Andy Rooney

" When I retire, I 'm going to spend my evenings by the fireplace going through those boxes. There are things in there that ought to be burned."   Richard Nixon

" A lot of people stop short. They don't actually die, but they say, ' Right, I'm old, and I am going to retire,' and then they dwindle into nothing. They go off to Florida and become jolly boring. " Mary Wesley

" The reason the pro tells you to keep your head down is so you can't see him laughing." Phyllis Diller

" The money's no better in retirement, but the hours are! " Terri Guillemets

Author Biography

Ray Matlock Smythe received a Bachelor of Arts degree in Education from Western Washington University in Bellingham, Washington. He received his Master of Arts degree in Teaching from Lewis and Clark College in Portland, Oregon. Mr. Smythe taught American history for 39 years in middle school and high school in Washington, Oregon, and California.

He has earned many accolades during his career. The three awards that were most meaningful to him were: being named the 1987 Portland Trailblazers Educator of the Year, being honored as the 2000 - 2001 Teacher of the Year at David Douglas High School, and having the Marywood Palm Valley School 2009 Yearbook dedicated to him the year he retired.

This is Mr. Smythe's third book. He previously published <u>So You Decided to Teach</u> and <u>One Card At a Time – Stories of Inspiration.</u>

He currently lives in Cathedral City, CA. Mr. Smythe may be reached at <u>Rayme49@aol.com</u>